The Pattern Library
EMBROIDERY

D0395744

The Pattern Library
EMBROIDERY

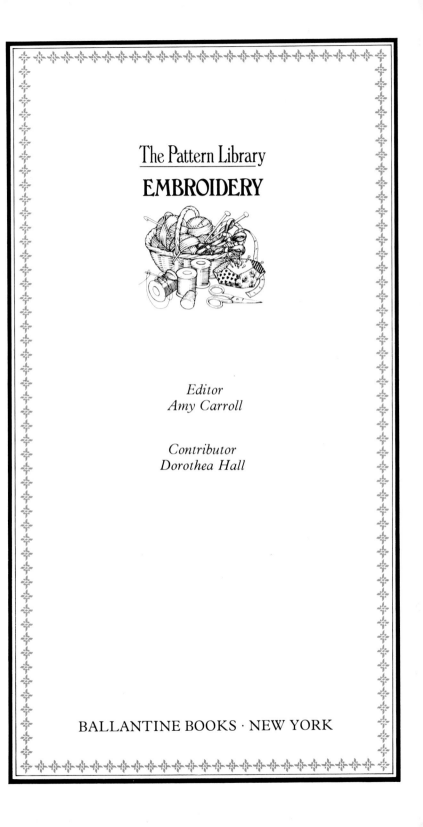

Editor
Amy Carroll

Contributor
Dorothea Hall

BALLANTINE BOOKS · NEW YORK

First published in Great Britain in 1981 by
Ebury Press, National Magazine House,
72 Broadwick Street, London W1V 2BP

The Pattern Library EMBROIDERY was conceived, edited
and designed by Dorling Kindersley Limited,
9 Henrietta Street, London WC2

Library of Congress Catalog Card Number: 81–66167

ISBN 0–345–29598–6

Manufactured in the United States of America

First Ballantine Books Edition: October 1981
10 9 8 7 6 5

Contents

❖

❖

Introduction

A study of embroideries from all over the world shows
that embroidery has served many different purposes and
satisfies a strong creative need – to embellish or decorate.
In some places it denotes rank, wealth and status (seen
particularly on clothes with religious or ceremonial significance),
while in other areas it may decorate a peasant girl's trousseau
or an everyday apron or rug, nonetheless lovingly
and patiently worked, often in incredibly difficult circumstances
from scant, home-spun materials.
The use of ground fabrics and threads of cotton, linen,
silk and wool is universal, as are many different design motifs,
symbols, stitches and colors. It is fascinating
to find that satin stitch, cross stitch, chain stitch and
straight stitch, together with their numerous variations, are
used almost throughout the world.
Though some designs and techniques such as English Jacobean
crewel work, Spanish blackwork and the silk
satin-stitched embroidery of China traveled with settlers or
followed trade routes, others did not. Local customs and
available raw materials characterize many ethnic
embroideries as in North American bead work and
Indian mirror work.
Through air travel, television and textile exhibitions
we are being made more and more aware of the beauty and many
delights of embroidery. Much embroidery worked
today is being done with great spontaneity, wit
and sometimes even drama. It is perhaps the most important
period ever for the individual embroiderer. Inspired by
its potential, top fashion designers have projected
embroidery still further, giving it a fresh youthful
image for many to see and enjoy.
The stitches and techniques in the book are grouped
into different "families" for easy reference.
Accompanied by clear stitch diagrams, fabric suggestions
and their practical uses, each illustration has been specially
selected to represent embroidery today.

THREADS

In addition to the threads listed below, many knitting, crochet and weaving yarns, raffia, macramé string, metallic and machine sewing threads may be used. Your choice of thread should, generally speaking, be governed by your choice of fabric and the purpose of your finished embroidery. In deciding, an important point to consider is whether or not your embroidery will be home-laundered, dry-cleaned or displayed behind glass. Embroidery threads are available in excellent ranges of fast-dyed colors and textures.

"**Filo-Floss**" is a soft, loosely-twisted, six-stranded pure silk thread; can be separated and used singly or in varying multiple strands as required.

Coton à broder is a single, highly-twisted thread with a shiny finish.

Pearl cotton is a single thread with a sharply-defined twist and shiny finish; available in plain and random-dyed colors.

Six-stranded cotton is a loosely-twisted mercerized thread with a light sheen, available in plain and random-dyed colors; can easily be separated into single strands and used in varying multiples, or in mixed colored strands, as required.

Linen thread is a very strong and tightly-twisted single thread with a slight lustrous finish.

Soft embroidery cotton is a single, fairly thick, soft thread with a matt finish.

Crewel wool is a very fine, firmly-twisted 2-ply yarn.

Metallic threads of pure gold and silver are tarnishable and need careful handling. Many imitations are available.

"Filo Floss" silk

linen thread

coton à broder

sewing threads

pearl cotton

six-stranded cotton

crewel wool

soft embroidery cotton

metallic threads

GROUND FABRICS

Almost any fabric can be embroidered, from very fine silk and muslin to leather, felt and flannel. Whether you wish to do surface embroidery, cross stitch, pulled work, or stitch on sequins and beads, you should choose a ground fabric that is suited to its purpose, the design and weight of thread used. In addition to the fabrics shown below, gingham check, spotted, striped, printed and knitted fabrics may all be used.

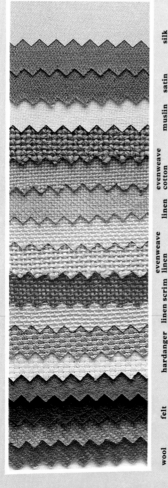

silk
satin
muslin
evenweave cotton
linen
evenweave linen
linen scrim
hardanger
felt
wool

NEEDLES

With the exception of pulled work, choose an embroidery needle with an eye large enough to hold the thread and small enough to pass easily through the fabric without distorting.

Crewel needles have sharp points with long oval eyes and should be used for all fine/medium surface embroidery.

Chenille needles have sharp points and oval eyes but are bigger than crewel needles; used for heavy threads and fabrics.

Tapestry needles have large oval eyes and round points; they should be used for pulled and drawn work.

Beading needles (straws) are long and very fine with a small eye; suitable for fine bead-work.

Sharps are strong, pointed needles with round eyes.

THIMBLE, SCISSORS AND PINS

Choose a well-fitting (stainless) metal thimble, and a pair of sharp, strong pointed scissors. Use fine dressmaker's steel pins and protect them from rusting by keeping a small square of specially prepared damp-absorbent paper in your pin box.

FRAMES

Embroidery frames are used to support the ground fabric while it is being worked. Though not always essential, their main advantage is that they keep the ground fabric evenly stretched, enabling the embroiderer to work even stitches. Those frames which can be fitted to a stand will also leave both hands free to work the stitches. For large pieces of work, choose a square or rectangular frame that can be supported, while smaller pieces of embroidery may be worked in a travel frame or ring (see p.10).

Straight-sided frames *are available in different sizes, measured across the roller tape. The standard straight-sided frame consists of two rollers (top and bottom), to which strips of tape or webbing are nailed, and two flat sides, which fit into slots on each roller and are held with pegs or screws.*

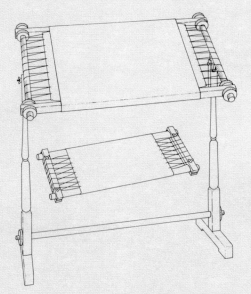

The travel frame *(inset) is light and portable. It is available in two 24in. (measured across the tape) by one standard depth of 12in.*

ATTACHING THE FABRIC TO THE FRAME

The way in which tension is put on a rectangular frame may vary depending on whether your frame has metal screws or wooden pegs, but the same method is used for attaching the ground fabric.

Begin by stitching a ½in. hem all round the fabric. On fine fabrics, stitch on tape to strengthen the side edges which are to be laced. Mark the center of both rollers and top and bottom edges of fabric.
1 *Matching center points, stitch fabric to webbing, working*

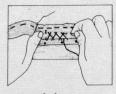

outwards from center. Roll excess fabric length around one roller. Attach sides, stretching fabric.

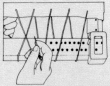

2 *Use linen thread to lace fabric evenly to side pieces. Tighten each side alternately and knot firmly.*

9

RING FRAMES

The ring frame is the most popular frame for working small areas of embroidery. Rings are available in various sizes, the simplest consisting of an outer and inner ring of wood, plastic or metal, fitting closely one within the other so that the fabric is kept evenly stretched. Others may have a screw attachment on the outer ring enabling the embroiderer to adjust tension on fine or thick fabrics. Ring frames can also be attached to a clamp.

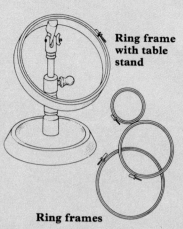

Ring frame with table stand

Ring frames

BINDING THE RING/STRETCHING THE FABRIC

To prevent the fabric from marking or slipping, you can bind the inner ring with tape before stretching the fabric.

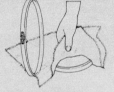

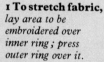

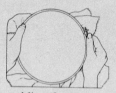

Bind inner ring *with 1in. woven tape (or bandage) and fasten with a few stitches.*

1 To stretch fabric, *lay area to be embroidered over inner ring; press outer ring over it.*

2 *Adjust the tension screw so that the fabric is smooth and the grain straight.*

RE-STRETCHING AND STRETCHING ODD SHAPES

Should you wish to work a long border pattern, you will need to move your ring and re-stretch the fabric as you finish each area, taking care not to damage the existing embroidery. Small cut sections are framed by first stitching them to a larger piece of fabric.

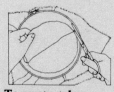

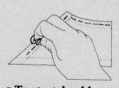

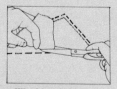

To re-stretch fabric, *lay next section over inner ring and cover with muslin. Secure outer ring and cut away muslin inside frame.*

1 To stretch odd shapes in a ring frame, *first sew the section(s) onto a larger supporting fabric and then stretch in usual way.*

2 *Working from the wrong side, cut away the supporting fabric from inside the shape, leaving it secured and ready for working.*

ENLARGING, REDUCING AND REPEATING DESIGNS

Existing designs can be enlarged or reduced and used in embroidery as all-over repeat patterns, borders or as single motifs. To do this, accurate measuring and correct positioning is vital. The enlarging procedure is shown below; for reducing, work in reverse order.

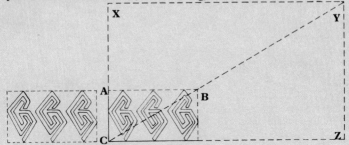

1 *Trace your design onto plain paper and enclose it with a rectangle. Lay design in bottom corner of large sheet of paper.*

Draw CBY. Extend CA and mark off chosen height at X. Draw XY parallel to CZ and complete enlargement with YZ.

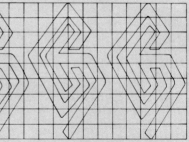

2 *Divide the original design into squares to form a grid. Then make the same number of squares in the*

larger rectangle. Copy the design from smaller to larger squares.

TRACING DESIGNS ONTO PAPER

Unless you have the outline of a design already printed onto your ground fabric you will need to know how one may be traced off onto paper from an existing pattern. The easiest way to do this is to use natural light through a window pane.

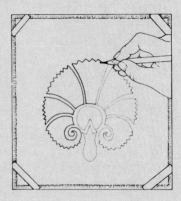

Attach the existing design to the inside of a window pane with masking tape. Similarly, attach a piece of tracing paper on top and, with apencil, trace off outline.

TRANSFERRING DESIGNS

In addition to commercially printed transfers there are various other methods you can use for transferring your own designs onto fabric. From the methods given below, select the one best suited to your ground fabric.

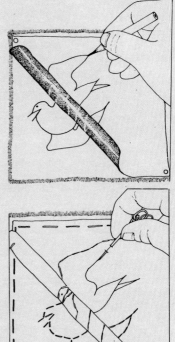

Dressmaker's carbon paper:
Suitable for smooth fabrics (use dark colors on light fabrics and vice versa). Lay carbon paper face down on fabric with traced design on top and draw around outline.

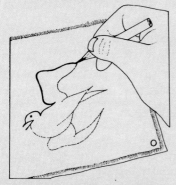

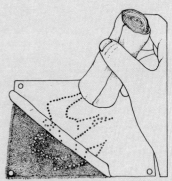

Basting through tissue paper:
Use for velvet and toweling. Pin lawn. Lay your fabric over the design and trace off with a pencil.

Basting through tissue paper:
Use for velvet and toweling. Pin design (on tissue paper) to fabric, outline and tear paper away.

Pouncing: *Use for transferring large designs to smooth fabrics.*
1 *Use a needle to prick around traced design.*

2 *Pin design to fabric. Dip felt pad into powdered chalk (charcoal for light fabrics) ; dab over holes. Lift paper and spray with fixative.*

PREPARING THE FABRIC FOR SMOCKING

Smocking is worked by gathering the fabric into even-size folds. It is always worked before the garment is assembled. The amount of fabric needed is usually about three times the actual finished width of the smocking, but less may be required if a thicker fabric is used. The position of the folds on the fabric is marked with the help of printed transfers, which have evenly spaced dots which are transferred onto the back of the fabric. Place on the straight grain.

1 *Using a knotted thread, bring the needle through and pick up a small piece of fabric at each dot. Leave gathering threads hanging loose.*

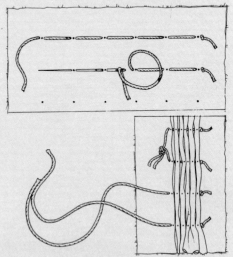

2 *Complete all the rows as above. Pull the loose ends up 1 row at a time, gathering the fabric to the required width. Tie the thread ends in pairs, stroking the gathers with a pin to even them out.*

PREPARING DRAWN THREAD BORDERS

These borders are worked by withdrawing either the warp or weft threads from an even weave fabric and then securing the remaining threads into decorative clusters to make regular patterns. Some clusters are prettily twisted with colored threads while others can be woven in stepped blocks of stitches, as in needleweaving. The edges of the borders are mostly hem-stitched while the depth can vary from a single withdrawn thread to really decorative borders measuring 2in. to 4in. deep.

To work a single border *across the width of the fabric, first measure, and, with a pin, mark its position on the fabric. First, withdraw one single thread right across the fabric width, and then withdraw any further threads as required, ready for embroidery.*

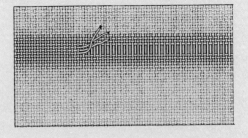

HOW TO DISPLAY YOUR EMBROIDERY

You may wish to have your large pieces of embroidery professionally framed under glass. For displaying small pictures, book covers or greetings cards use the display method shown below.

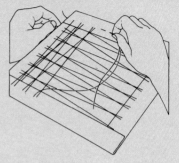

For work larger than 12in. square, use hardboard backing and cardboard for all smaller pieces. Turn embroidery face down with cardboard on top. Fold over fabric margins on two opposite sides and lace back and forth with strong thread. Lace the other two sides and, finally, pull stitches to tighten.

USEFUL TIPS

Before working: It is always best to work a trial piece first, testing the thickness of thread and stitch to fabric.

Choosing threads and fabrics: A simple rule to remember is to use silk on silk, cotton on cotton and synthetic on synthetic and so on.

Calculating fabric: In calculating how much fabric you will need, add an extra 2in. all round for handling and stretching.

Finishing off: Avoid using knots. Not only do they make pressing the embroidery difficult, they show up as shiny areas when pressed. Where possible, run starting end through fabric under the area to be worked. Finish on the wrong side by running the end under stitches just worked.

Working embroidery on garments: Remember to work the embroidery before cutting out the pattern pieces, when very little pressing will be needed.

Pressing embroidery: Press all embroidery on a well-padded board. For linen, cotton and wool, press on wrong side of the fabric under a damp cloth.

Iron-on transfer: Should you wish to use an iron-on transfer for your design, set the thermostat on your iron to "cotton" (necessary heat for a good impression) and test on a scrap piece of fabric. Some synthetic fabrics are unsuitable for iron-on transfers (see p.12).

FLAT STITCHES

Included in this group of stitches are some of the easiest of all stitches to work, such as back stitch and straight stitch, and also some that are not easy. A little preliminary practice is needed to get the beautiful smooth finish and sharp edges of satin stitch and the subtle shading in long and short stitch. Here the diagonal threads lie close to the surface catching and reflecting light, and contrasting strongly with the simple lines of stem and running stitches, through leafy filling stitches and pattern darning to the spontaneous needlepainting effect of straight stitch.

Back stitch

Materials Stranded silk or cotton, or 6 strands of mixed sewing threads for a sharp sporty look; soft embroidery or crewel wool for chunkier outline.

Uses Simple motif for T-shirt, tracksuit, or blazer "badge"; blouson, scarf or sports bag.

Bring the thread through on the stitch line, then make a small backward stitch. Take needle forward under the fabric to emerge one stitch length ahead, ready to make the next stitch. Keep all stitches small and even.

Stem stitch

Materials Stranded silk or cotton, sewing threads or fine pearl thread for quick, fun filling and feature lines.

Uses Motif for sweatshirt, jeans or greetings card; enlarge, or repeat, for child's duvet and pillow.

For a single line, work from left to right along the stitch line. Keeping thread to the left of the needle, make small, even stitches. Work infilled areas in the same way, where each row should follow the outline shape.

Wide stem stitch

Materials Silk, pearl or mixed stranded cotton for firm outlining.
Uses Motif for greetings card, sweater, shirt, dress bodice, or shoulder bag; all-over repeat or border for bolero, skirt hem or cushion set.

Work as for stem stitch, opposite, but insert the needle into the ground fabric at a slight angle. For a wider, rope-like effect, increase the angle of the stitch.

Satin stitch

Materials Stranded silk or cotton, pearl or soft embroidery thread for a really smooth finish.

Uses Motif for karate jacket, sports towel or bath robe; monogram for dressing gown, bed linen, sports bag or tracksuit.

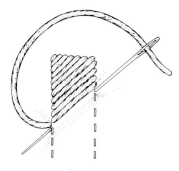

Work straight stitches diagonally across the area to be filled. The stitches should fit closely together, all at the same angle, and form straight outside edges to the embroidered shapes.

Horizontal satin stitch

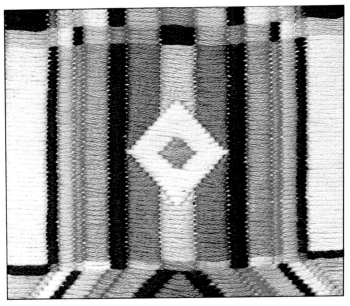

Materials Stranded silk or cotton, pearl or mixed strands of sewing threads for clear, geometric infilling.
Uses All-over pattern for dress yoke or inset panel, clutch bag flap, cuff or pocket detail, or cushion set border.

For best results, work horizontal straight stitches on evenweave fabric. The stitches should fit closely together, giving a very smooth surface and straight outside edges.

Double running stitch

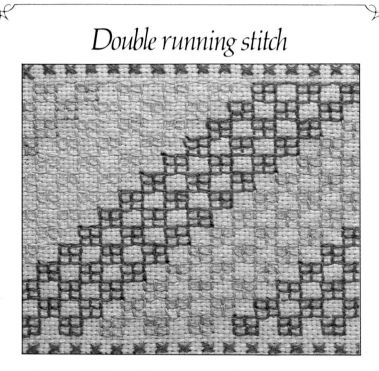

Materials Medium-weight pearl, coton à broder or stranded cotton for a very pretty geometric pattern on evenweave fabric.
Uses Dress bodice inset panel, pocket or purse detail; deep border for cushion set, pillow cover, buffet runner or trolley cloth.

Working from right to left, make small stitches, the same length as the space between, along the outline of the design. Make a return journey from left to right, filling in the spaces left between.

Fishbone stitch

Materials Silk, pearl or stranded cotton for a neat, naturalistic effect.

Uses Motif for nightdress or négligé, bed linen, table linen or wall-hanging; stitch sampler.

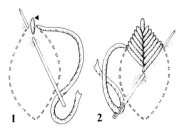

1 *Make a small straight stitch at tip of central line.*
2 *Follow with overlapping filling stitches, sloping alternately to one side and then the other.*

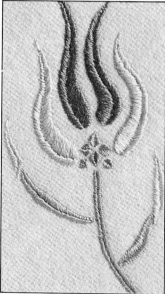

Open fishbone stitch

Materials Silk, stranded cotton, pearl or fine lurex thread for a light, leafy filling.

Uses Motif for dress shoulder, evening wrap or shawl border; greetings card, book cover, or padded jewel-box lid panel.

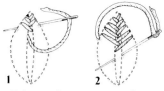

1 *Bring needle out at arrow. Insert to right, carry thread across back, and bring out at left.*
2 *Make sloping stitch to right and repeat step 1.*

Darning stitch

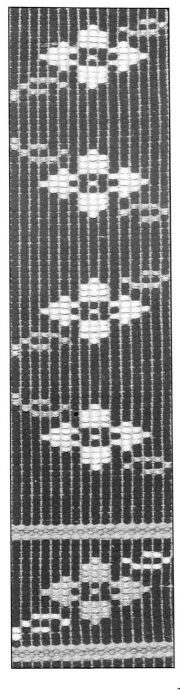

Materials Stranded cotton, pearl or soft embroidery thread for a pretty, yet simple pattern on evenweave fabric.

Uses Border for bolero, belt, or suspenders; all-over pattern for shoulder bag, purse, guest towel or cushion set.

Working on evenweave fabric, make a series of darning stitches to form a ribbed pattern. First, work a row of equal-sized darning stitches, picking up 1 thread between each stitch. Work the next and subsequent rows directly under the first, in the colors of your chosen pattern.

Long and short stitch

Materials Fine to medium-stranded silk or cotton for delicate shading; soft embroidery thread, crewel wool or tapestry yarn for a chunky look.

Uses Motif for collar or pocket detail or repeat pattern for picture frame border; cushion set, bolster bands or bell-pull.

Work the first row in alternate long and short satin stitches, closely following the outline of the shape. Work all subsequent rows in satin stitches of equal length, choosing an appropriately colored thread to give a shaded effect.

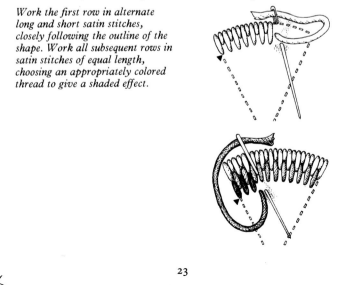

Straight stitch

Materials Silk, coton à broder, stranded or pearl cotton for an easy-to-work grassy effect; lurex, soft embroidery, crewel or tapestry wool for chunky needlepainting.

Uses Anniversary card, or keepsake picture; dress yoke, shawl corner motif, cushion inset panel or border repeat.

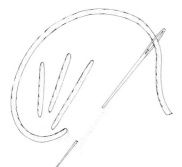

Shown as single spaced stitches, straight stitches may be worked evenly, irregularly, long, short or overlapping. The stitches should be neither too loose nor too long so as to snag.

CROSSED STITCHES

These are some of the most popular of all embroidery stitches. They can be worked evenly by counting the warp and weft threads of the ground fabric or they can be stitched individually and completely at random, bearing in mind that the regular appearance of any crossed stitch is made by crossing all the stitches in the same direction. The different textures of crossed stitches vary enormously from the woven effect of a background filling and plaited band to the softness of shadow stitch and the spotted repeat of St George cross and star stitch filling.

Long=armed cross stitch

Materials Medium-weight pearl, cotton or linen thread for bold geometric background filling on coarse evenweave fabric.
Uses Border for floor-cushion set, curtain, bed cover or bolster, or stitch sampler for patchwork cushion or quilt.

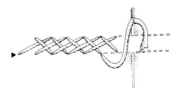 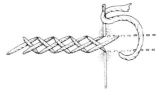

1 *Starting at arrow, insert needle up to right, making a long diagonal stitch, and bring out directly below.*

2 *Make a short diagonal stitch. Insert needle up to left and bring out below, ready for next stitch.*

25

Cross stitch

1 *To work small areas of color in cross stitch, individual crosses are made in 2 steps as shown. Bring thread out at top left, insert needle diagonally to bottom right and bring out an equal distance above.*
2 *Make a diagonal stitch down to left and bring needle out at the top ready to make the next stitch.*

Materials Stranded cotton or pearl thread for creating realistic motifs on evenweave linen.
Uses Repeat motif for table linen, buttoned napkin ring, or trolley cloth, curtain ties or pillow cover.

"Assisi" cross stitch

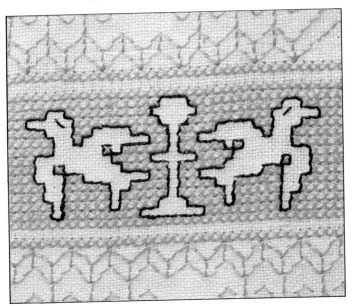

Materials Stranded silk, or cotton, coton à broder, or pearl thread for intricate background patterning on evenweave linen.

Uses Border for placemat, tray or trolley cloth, table linen or towel; stitch sampler or patchwork quilt module.

In Assisi work, cross stitches are worked to fill the background area, leaving the motif unworked; this may be outlined with back stitch or double running stitch.

1 Working from right to left, first make a row of even diagonal stitches.

2 Then work back again, with the upper half of the cross pointing from bottom left to top right, as shown.

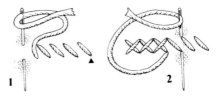

Ermine stitch

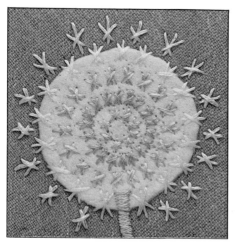

Work a long, straight stitch and cover with an elongated cross stitch, placed just above the base of the straight stitch, as shown in the diagram.

Materials Medium-weight stranded cotton or pearl thread for a pretty, versatile filling stitch.

Uses Motif for egg-cosy set, greetings card or keepsake picture; extend motif to coffee-pot cosy or wall panel.

St George cross stitch

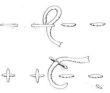

First, work a row of evenly-spaced, horizontal stitches and then cross each one with a stitch of equal length.

Materials Fine to medium-weight silk or cotton thread, for a delicate filling stitch.

Uses Corner motif for cushion set, headsquare, neck-tie, cravat or handkerchief, pocket or purse flap.

Open Cretan stitch

Materials Silk, sewing thread, coton à broder or stranded cotton for delicate outlining.

Uses Motif for keepsake picture, greetings card or toddler's dress yoke; border repeat for cushion set, matching duvet and pillow set or child's nightdress.

Work short vertical stitches alternately downwards and upwards, with the working thread held down to the right under the needle. This stitch may also be worked slightly closer together for infilling.

Closed herringbone stitch

Materials Medium-weight pearl thread, coton à broder, stranded silk or cotton for a rich, textured effect.

Uses Deep border pattern for bedspread, and matching pillows, evening wrap; party dress bodice, clutch bag or cape.

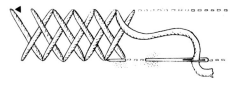

Starting from the left, make a row of interlaced diagonal stitches by working small back stitches alternately on each side of a traced double line.

Shadow stitch

Materials Fine stranded silk or cotton, mixed sewing thread or coton à broder for delicate, shadowy effect on sheer fabric.
Uses Dress or shirt inset panel, sleeve or hem detail; nightdress or négligé trim, baby's carriage set or lampshade.

This stitch is the reverse side of closed herringbone stitch, opposite. Work on the right side of sheer fabric, where the color of the herringbone shows through, in a delicate way. Starting from the right, work small back stitches, alternately on each side of the double lines. Dotted lines show the formation of the thread on wrong side of fabric.

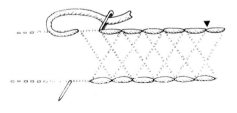

Ladder stitch

Materials 8-stranded cotton, coton à broder, pearl or soft embroidery thread for simple initialling.

Uses Centre back motif for judo jacket, tracksuit top, blazer pocket, canvas director's chair back, sports towel or pet's towel.

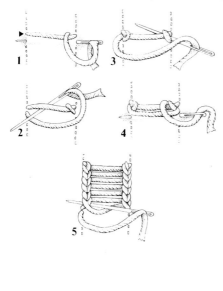

1 *Beginning at arrow, make small stitch to right and cross with 2nd small stitch, inserting needle at outside edge; pass behind and bring out just under starting point.*
2 *Without piercing fabric slip needle under 1st "rung" of ladder.*
3 *Pass needle under knot at right.*
4 *Insert needle at outside edge, pass behind and bring through as before.*
5 *Pass needle through plait on left and repeat steps 4 and 5 to complete ladder.*

Chevron stitch

Materials Pearl thread, coton à broder or stranded cotton for a simple pictorial effect.

Uses "My house" motif, picture or greetings card; "house"-shaped tea-cosy, coffee-pot cosy, work bag, or 3-dimensional "sculpture".

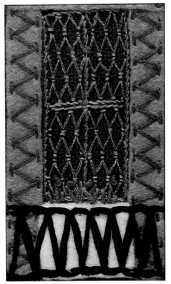

Bring thread out on lower line and make a short stitch forward and a half stitch back. Work a similar stitch on the upper line a little to the right. First make a short stitch to left then one of equal size to right and continue to work alternately from one side to the other.

Vandyke stitch

Material Coton à broder, pearl, stranded silk or cotton for a neat leafy filling.

Uses Spot motif for négligé or petticoat, or repeat motif for table linen or cushion border; motif for suede waistcoat, leather belt or bag, slipper fronts or espadrilles.

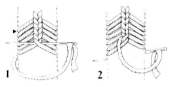

1 *With thread at arrow, make small horizontal stitch at center, insert needle to right and bring through just below starting point. Without piercing fabric, pass needle under crossed thread.*
2 *Insert to right and bring through at left side, ready to make next stitch.*

33

Star filling stitch

Materials Fine to medium-weight stranded silk or cotton, sewing threads or pearl cotton for decorative filling on padded appliqué.
Uses Motif for leather belt or bag, blouson, bolero or hatband; repeat motif applied to fabric patchwork quilt or cushion set.

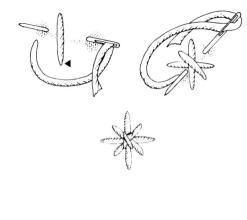

First, make upright cross stitch and then work an equal-sized diagonal cross stitch on top, finishing with a tiny central cross as shown. Each cross may be worked in a different color.

LOOPED STITCHES

Many of the stitches made by looping the thread either under or over the needle can be fairly broad and therefore cover the ground fabric reasonably quickly. Braids and other border stitches may be opened or closed in working depending on whether you want a firm band effect or a softer outlining. Remember that the loops of a broad braid will stay flat and keep their shape if they are worked in a firm thread. Here, a great variety of stitches range from twisted, chain and zigzag lines through fast buttonhole infillings and bold braided borders to single spaced chains.

Daisy stitch

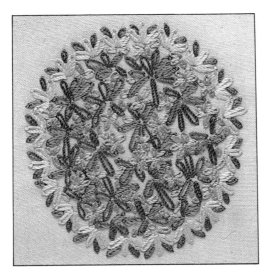

Materials Stranded silk or cotton, pearl or coton à broder for a pretty lacy filling; tapestry or baby wool for knitwear.
Uses Motif for baby's dress and jacket or toddler's nightdress; baby's carriage set, or all-over repeat for carrying cape or cot-cover.

With thread at arrow, hold down to left and insert needle at starting point. Bring out, a short distance away, with thread under needle. Insert needle under loop; make a tying stitch.

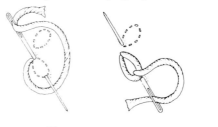

Chain stitch

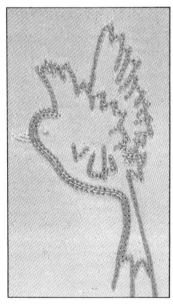

Materials Fine stranded silk or cotton, or sewing thread for fine line detail; linen thread or soft embroidery for heavy-duty wear.
Uses Motif for light summer dress, neck and pocket detail, bride's purse, négligé or petticoat; jeans and jacket motif.

Hold thread down to left at arrow. Insert needle at starting point and bring out a short distance below with thread under needle. Pull through, ready for next stitch.

Zigzag chain stitch

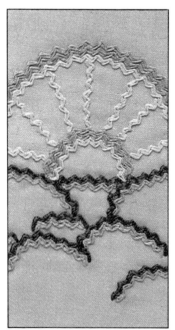

Materials Pearl or stranded cotton for easy-to-work landscape effect; soft embroidery or tapestry wool for outlining.
Uses Child's dress yoke or inset panel, egg-cosy set; school satchel or shoulder bag motif.

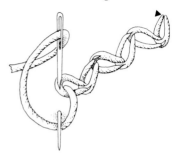

Work as chain stitch but make each one at an angle to previous one, piercing loop as new stitch is made.

Rosette chain stitch

Materials Medium-weight silk, pearl or cotton thread for decorative outlining; soft embroidery or tapestry wool for a chunky braid effect.

Uses Repeat motif for bride's dress inset panel, keepsake picture or anniversary card; denim skirt or bolero border.

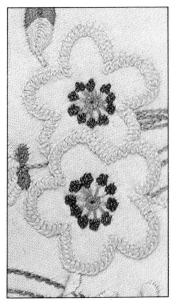

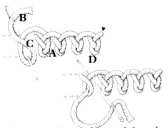

With thread at A, loop to left and hold down. Insert needle at B and pull through at C. Pass needle under thread at D

Chequered chain stitch

Materials 6-stranded cotton, pearl or soft embroidery thread for simple diagonal stripes.

Uses Repeat pattern across dress yoke, and pocket detail, cushion corner, crib or carriage set.

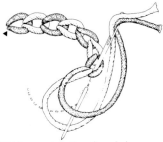

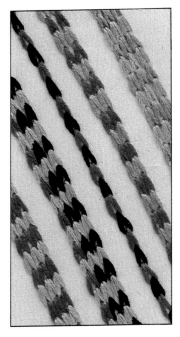

With 2 contrasting threads in needle, make alternate chain stitches, keeping thread not in use above needle point.

Double chain stitch

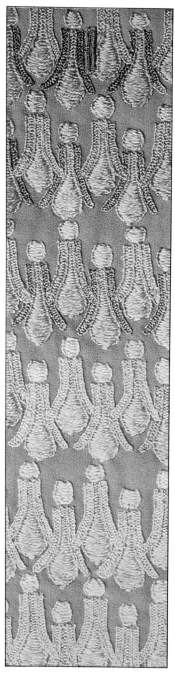

Materials Stranded silk or cotton, coton à broder or fine lurex thread for pretty shaped filling.
Uses All-over pattern for dress yoke, cuff and pocket detail, evening dress inset panel or shawl corner and matching clutch bag.

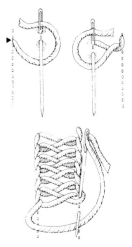

Bring thread out at arrow. Make small vertical stitch to right with thread looped under needle. Then make a similar stitch to the left as shown. Continue in this way, working subsequent stitches into loops of previous chains.

Tamboured chain stitch

Materials Medium-weight silk, pearl, or stranded cotton for all-over flowery pattern; crewel wool, tapestry or knitting yarn for heavy-duty fabrics.

Uses All-over repeat for herb-filled pillow, cushion set, waistcoat or shawl border; repeat motif for bedspread, slippers or tote-bag.

Working in a frame, with right side of fabric uppermost, and with a fine hook, knot end of working thread and hold it underneath. Insert hook downwards and draw thread through to form a loop. With loop on hook, insert a short distance away and on stitch line, and draw through another loop. Draw second loop through first to form a chain stitch and continue.

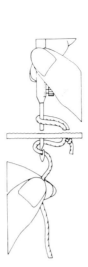

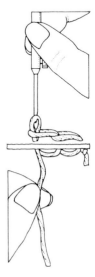

Twisted chain stitch

Materials Stranded silk or cotton for a firm, corded effect; soft embroidery or crewel wool for chunkier outlining.

Uses Initialled sportswear, bath robe, dressing gown or satin purse; blazer "badge", blouson or shoulder bag motif.

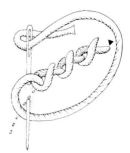

Hold thread to left at arrow.
Insert needle to left of thread.
Make diagonal stitch on stitch line.

Buttonhole stitch

Materials Coton à broder, pearl or stranded cotton for a rainbow look; soft embroidery or tapestry yarn for heavier fabrics.

Uses Sweatshirt, T-shirt or blouson motif; sports bag, towel or canvas espadrille decoration.

Working from left to right, bring needle out at arrow. Hold thread to right and make a downward vertical stitch, bringing needle out over thread.

Up and down buttonhole stitch

Materials Silk thread, stranded or pearl cotton for light-weight infilling; soft embroidery or crewel wool for fine knitteds.

Uses Kimono sash motif, dressing gown lapel, jumpsuit or bag initial; sweater, mitts, hat or scarf motif.

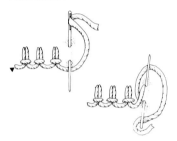

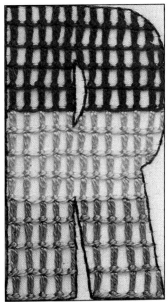

Make a buttonhole stitch. Insert needle upwards into same holes with thread under point. Pull through.

Closed buttonhole stitch

Materials Coton à broder, sewing threads, silk or stranded cotton for a bright, jewel-like effect.

Uses Motif for cotton blazer lapel, waistcoat front or diagonal repeat for dress bodice.

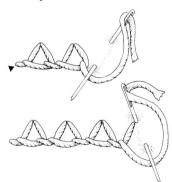

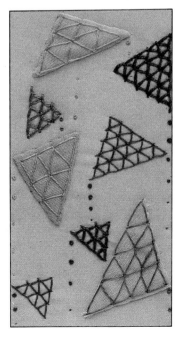

Work pairs of buttonhole stitches into same hole to form triangles, as shown.

Wheatear stitch

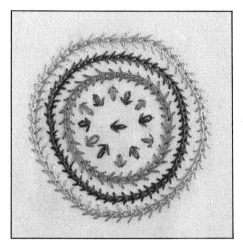

Work stitches AB. With needle at C pass under threads. Insert at C to emerge at left.

Materials Coton à broder, stranded silk or cotton for delicate infilling; soft embroidery or crewel wool for a chunkier look.

Uses Motif for baby's pram set, toddler's dress yoke, or bride's purse; border motif for flannel vest or skirt.

Fly stitch

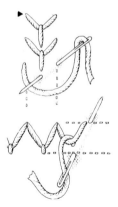

Holding thread downwards, make diagonal stitch to center. Make tying stitch.

Materials Sewing threads, stranded silk or cotton for a fine powdery filling; soft embroidery cotton or raffia for a chunky look.

Uses Motif for toddler's or baby's dress yoke, carriage pillow or cot-cover; repeat pattern for ribbon-trimmed straw hat brim.

Braid stitch

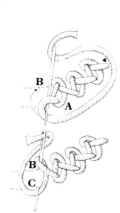

With thread at A, hold to left. Pass needle under loop, twist up into B to emerge at C.

Materials Pearl or 8-stranded cotton, soft embroidery or crewel wool for a chunky trim; silk or lurex thread for added sparkle.

Uses Border for bath robe, blazer cuff, skirt hem or vest front; evening wrap, purse, dress sash or floating panel.

Cretan stitch

Holding thread to left at arrow, make a small stitch down to center with thread under needle point as shown. Make a similar stitch to left and continue.

Materials Medium-weight silk, pearl or stranded cotton, or tapestry wool for a bold, woven texture.

Uses Deep border for sofa valance and matching bolster, curtain or cushion set.

Single feather stitch

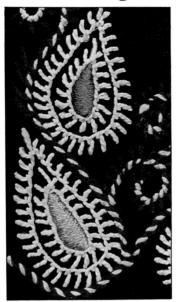

Materials Coton à broder, pearl, stranded or soft embroidery cotton for a bright country look.

Uses Dress yoke and cuffs; border for placemat, buffet runner, curtain ties or apron.

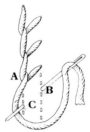

Bring needle out at A. With thread held to left, insert at B and bring out at C, with loop under needle.

Feather stitch

Materials Coton à broder, pearl or stranded cotton for a simple decorative finish.

Uses Peasant blouse inset panel and cuffs, border repeat for cushion set, apron, egg-cosy set, bag or belt.

Begin with a single feather stitch. Make a similar stitch to the left, on the same level, and continue working these two movements alternately.

KNOTTED STITCHES

*This group of stitches has an interesting range of stitch
textures, from the tiniest single dot used in spotted
backgrounds and shaded clusters, to long bullion twists,
through sharp sword-like stitches, textured lines and
broad trellis infilling. The secret of making knots,
whether you wish to work them singly to soften harder
edges of your embroidery, or as long twisted coils, is to
hold the working thread firmly while the needle twists
around it, and to continue holding the knot in place until
you have passed your needle to the back to secure it.*

French knot

Materials Linen thread, pearl or stranded cotton, soft embroidery
or crewel wool for a well-raised effect; silk or fine sewing thread for
light-textured powdering.
Uses Keepsake picture or cushion set; anniversary card or padded
jewel-box lid panel.

*Holding thread down with left
thumb, encircle thread twice with
needle. Then twist needle back to
arrow and insert it close to starting
point. Pull through to back before
repositioning for next stitch.*

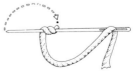

Bullion knot

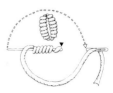

Pick up fabric same size as required bullion knot, but do not pull needle through. Twist thread several times round small-eyed needle. Hold coils, pull needle through and turn back to insert at starting point.

Materials Silk or linen thread, pearl, plain or random-dyed cotton for a bold chunky texture.

Uses Motif for bed linen, window blind or lapel badge; repeat pattern for dress yoke, hatband or bridesmaid's sash.

Four=legged knot stitch

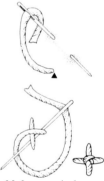

Make a vertical stitch, and bring needle out ready to make the upper cross. Hold thread to left; pass needle under stitch and thread. Complete cross.

Materials Coton à broder, stranded cotton or linen thread for a bright, geometric filling.

Uses Single or repeat motif for table linen, trolley cloth, buffet runner, napkin ring or dress inset panel.

Sword edge stitch

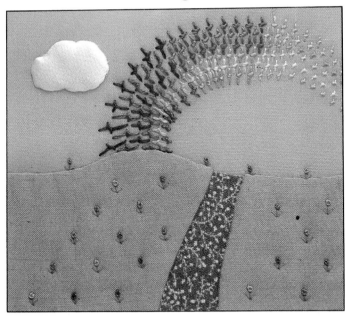

Materials Fine to medium silk, sewing threads, coton à broder or stranded cotton for rainbow-shaded filling.

Uses Motif for keepsake picture, greetings card, silk blouson back panel or dress pocket detail.

Bring the needle out at A, insert at B and bring out again at C; do not pull this stitch too tight. Pass the needle under the stitch, insert at D and bring out at E, ready to work the next stitch.

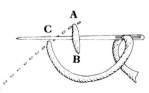

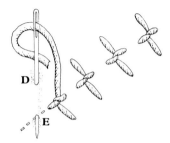

Diamond stitch

Materials Medium-weight stranded cotton, pearl or soft embroidery thread for a colorful geometric pattern.

Uses Single line border for bath robe or trolley cloth; deep border for cushion set, towel or bed cover.

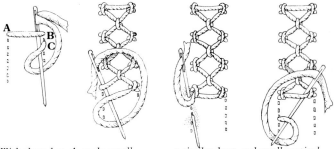

With thread at A, make small vertical stitch at BC. Hold thread to left, pass needle under stitch and working thread to form knot, make

a similar knot and small vertical stitch at left. Work a knot in center as shown and continue in this way.

Coral stitch

Materials Fine silk, sewing threads, coton à broder or stranded cotton for a pretty, outlining effect.
Uses Motif for birthday or wedding anniversary card, keepsake picture or cushion inset panel.

Hold thread to left. Make a small sloping stitch a short distance away, inserting needle under stitch line and thread. Bring needle out over lower thread as shown.

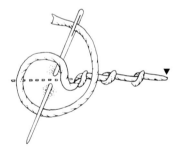

Double knot stitch

Materials Medium to heavy-weight silk or stranded cotton for raised, decorative outlining.
Uses Tree motif for satin wall-hanging, center panel for bedspread, cushion set or kimono back.

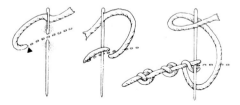

Working from left to right, first make small stitch across stitch line. Then pass needle downwards under stitch and pull through. Repeat, looping thread under needle point. Pull thread through to form a knot. Keep the knots evenly spaced along the stitch line.

COMPOSITE STITCHES

Some of the most ornamental stitch patterns with strong color combinations are included in this group of stitches. Most composite stitches can successfully be worked to give a deep embossed effect by lacing with heavy threads which might otherwise not easily go through the ground fabric. Use a round-pointed needle for lacing embroidery thread, cord or metallic threads and a ribbon threader for inserting fine braid or ribbon (see cloud filling stitch, p.53), remembering also to keep the foundation stitch for interlacing fairly loose. Here, extensive stitch patterns range from a simple line of whipped stitches through loopy fillings and bold decorative borders to the fascinating interlaced pattern of Maltese cross.

Pekinese stitch

Materials Medium to heavy-weight stranded silk or cotton, pearl or soft embroidery thread for colorful outlining and infilling.
Uses Motif for kimono inset panel, obi sash, evening bag or satin cushion set.

Work a foundation row of back stitch, and then, working from the left, interlace it with the same or a second colored thread.

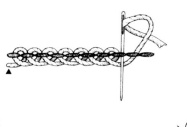

Whipped stem stitch

Materials Silk thread, pearl or stranded cotton for a two-tone twisted outline; soft embroidery, crewel wool or tapestry yarn for a heavy corded effect.

Uses Motif for pictorial picture panel, lampshade or greetings card; floor cushion panel or window blind motif.

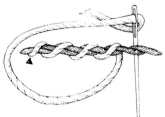

Work a foundation row of stem stitch first, and, with a second color, whip over the stitches without picking up the ground fabric, as shown.

Threaded back stitch

Materials Medium-weight stranded cotton, pearl or soft embroidery thread, or tapestry yarn for a rich, nubbly outline.

Uses Initialled bath robe, necktie, pet's cushion or towel.

Work a foundation row of back stitch. Then thread through 2 contrasting colors in separate journeys without picking up ground fabric, as shown.

Cloud filling stitch

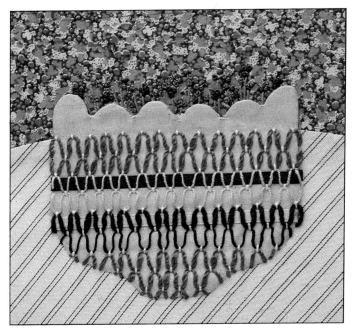

Materials Medium-weight silk, pearl or cotton thread (with narrow ribbon) for a decorative filling.
Uses Keepsake picture, or greetings card motif; cushion inset panel, or single module for patchwork quilt.

Work a foundation row of small vertical stitches regularly placed as shown. Begin at arrow and with a second colored thread, lace through, taking it first under an upper stitch and then under a lower one. Narrow ribbon may also be threaded under the stitching.

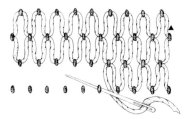

Guilloche stitch

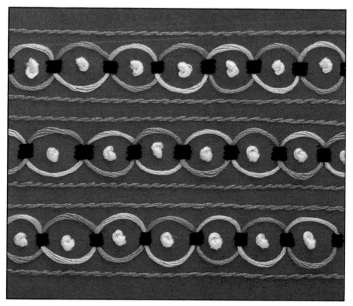

Materials Stranded cotton, soft embroidery thread, crewel wool or tapestry yarn for a striking border pattern.
Uses Floor-cushion set, bolster bands or patchwork stitch sampler; skirt hem, napkin ring set, belt or suspenders.

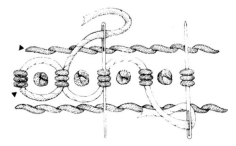

Work the 2 outer lines of the border in stem stitch first. Then work groups of 3 satin stitches evenly spaced and lace 2 contrasting colored threads in 2 journeys. Finish circles with french knot.

Laced herringbone stitch

Materials Medium-weight stranded silk or cotton, lurex or soft embroidery threads for an intricate, ethnic look.

Uses Border for kaftan neck, sleeve or hem; belt, suspenders, picture frame, or patchwork insertion.

Work the foundation row of herringbone stitch upside-down. With a contrasting thread, begin to lace, making 2 complete circles around each upper cross and one and a half around each lower cross.

Maltese cross stitch

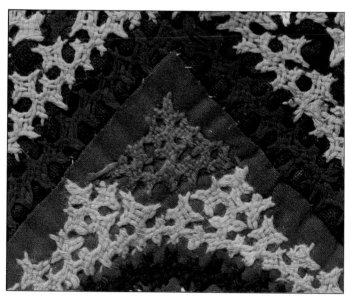

Materials Medium-weight pearl or stranded cotton, soft embroidery thread, or crewel wool for very decorative interlacing.

Uses Vest inset panel; dressing gown or cushion set border or stitch sampler square for patchwork quilt.

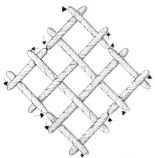

1 *Starting at large arrow, work a framework of crossed and interlaced threads, as shown.*

2 *Starting at center arrow lace each cross as 4 separate sections. Complete the cross and take needle to back before repositioning for next cross.*

SMOCKING STITCHES

This form of embroidery includes stitches that are both practical and pretty. By working over the small folds of evenly gathered fabric, it is fairly easy to regulate the size of your stitching. In smocking, extra fabric is required (see p.13), and the correct stitch should be chosen to give the right amount of control and elasticity. Though traditionally worked in matching colored threads, these pretty stitch patterns include rope, cable, lattice, honeycomb and wavy line effects embroidered in contrasting colors.

Rope stitch

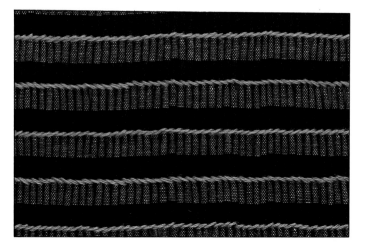

Materials Coton à broder, pearl, or stranded cotton for a light, banded effect on patterned fabric.

Uses Dress yoke, and pocket detail, blouson saddle and cuffs, summer-skirt band and pouch bag or all-over pattern for cushion.

A firm control stitch : bring needle up through first fold on left. With thread above needle, work stem stitch across row, picking up small pieces of fabric on each fold. To work stitch in opposite direction, keep thread below needle as shown.

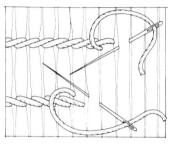

Single cable stitch

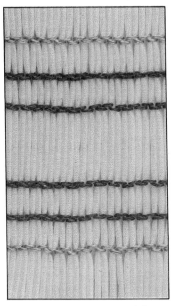

Materials Coton à broder, pearl or stranded cotton for a raised banded pattern.

Uses Summer dress pocket and bag detail, kitchen curtain heading, or bedspread valance.

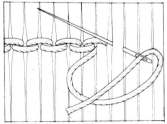

A firm control stitch : bring needle up through first fold on left, and draw through next fold. Work with thread above needle for one stitch and below for next, to end of row.

Double cable stitch

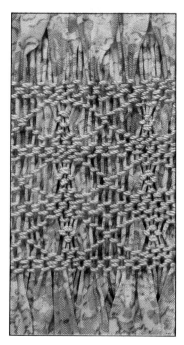

Materials Coton à broder, pearl or stranded cotton for a deep diamond border.

Uses Child's dress yoke and pocket detail or curtain heading; all-over pattern for sundress bodice and matching bag or cushion set.

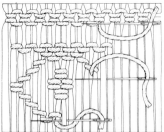

Work 2 rows of cable stitch evenly spaced across the area to be smocked. Then work 2 rows of wave stitch to form a trellis pattern joined by 5 horizontal cable stitches. Finish by adding 4 single cable stitches to center of diamonds.

Vandyke smocking stitch

Materials Stranded silk or cotton, coton à broder or pearl thread for a traditional look.

Uses Deep banded yoke for smock, baby's dress, or pajama wrist and ankle cuff.

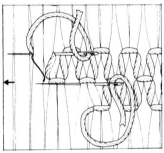

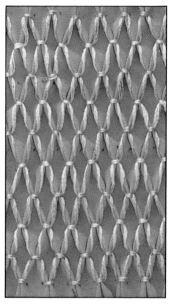

With thread at arrow, backstitch 1st and 2nd folds with thread above needle. Take needle down to 2nd line, backstitch 2nd and 3rd folds with thread below needle.

Double closed wave stitch

Materials Pearl, coton à broder, silk thread or stranded cotton for a pretty wavy pattern.

Uses All-over repeat for cushion set, curtain heading, bed valance or girl's dress bodice, pocket and sleeve detail.

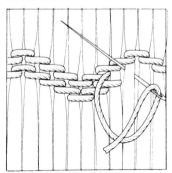

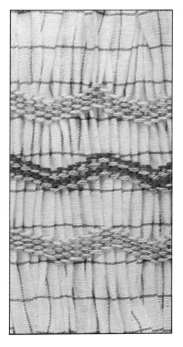

A firm control stitch: work 2 rows of wave stitch in zigzag pattern as required. Keep thread below needle when working upwards and above needle when working downwards.

Honeycomb stitch

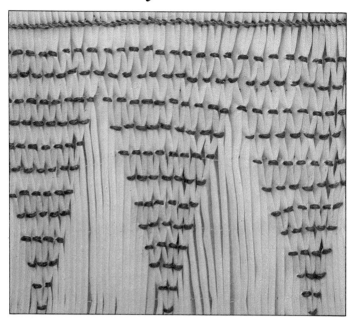

Materials Stranded silk or cotton, pearl or coton à broder for very dainty gathering.

Uses Dress yoke, and cuffs, shirt or smock saddle and sleeve detail, baby's crib drapes or bedroom curtain heading.

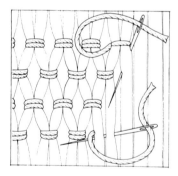

Work from left to right. Bring needle out on 1st line and back-stitch 2nd and 1st folds together twice. Slip needle behind fold to emerge at 2nd fold on line below. Backstitch 3rd and 2nd folds together twice. Return needle to 1st line at 3rd fold and draw 4th and 3rd folds together as before. Continue working alternately up and down to end of row. Work next and following rows in same way.

Surface honeycomb stitch

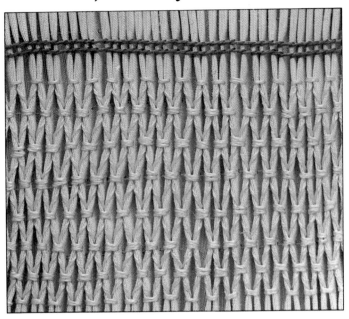

Materials Coton à broder, pearl or stranded cotton, or linen threads for a traditional gathering pattern.

Uses Mixed stitch shirt or smock yoke, sleeve inset panel or cuff, or pajama wrist and ankle detail.

Work in a similar way to honeycomb stitch, opposite, but keep working thread on the surface of the fold, and instead of making 2 back stitches, have thread emerge from center of back stitch before moving on to next stitch. Make sure thread is correctly positioned either above or below the needle.

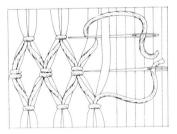

Diamond stitch

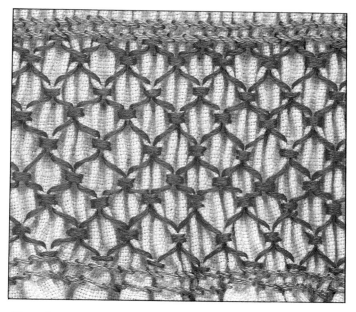

Materials Medium-stranded silk or cotton, coton à broder or pearl thread for a lattice effect.

Uses Child's dress yoke, bolster bands, tunic yoke and cuff detail; all-over pattern for carriage cover, cotton pouch bag, set of long cushions or bed valance heading.

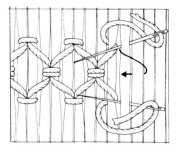

A very elastic stitch: work from left to right. Bring needle out on 2nd line then take it up on 1st line, backstitch 1st fold and then the 2nd fold with thread above needle. Take needle down to 2nd line, backstitch 3rd fold and repeat on 4th, with thread below needle. Take needle up to 5th fold and repeat from 1st fold. To shape diamond, start second stage on 3rd line. The completed diamond should have 2 folds in center.

PULLED & DRAWN

Both pulled and drawn thread techniques are best worked on an evenweave fabric, using a round-pointed needle, so as to pass easily between and without piercing the threads of the ground fabric. The delicate effects of pulled stitch patterns show up more clearly on loosely woven fabric, while drawn thread patterns are emphasized by decorating and twisting together small clusters of loose warp or weft threads (see p.13). This group of stitches offers the widest range of decorative textures, from very subtle circular movements and radiating stars through crossed and knotted clusters to interwoven bars.

Honeycomb darning stitch

Materials Coton à broder, stranded cotton or linen thread for pattern pulling strength and firm outlining.
Uses Dress yoke or pocket detail, linen blazer badge, placemat or napkin; all-over repeat for pillow border or cushion set.

Bring thread out at arrow; insert needle 3 horizontal threads down and bring out 3 vertical threads to left. Insert up over 3 horizontal threads and bring out 3 vertical threads to left. Continue to end of row. Work subsequent groups into the base of the previous ones.

Indian drawn ground

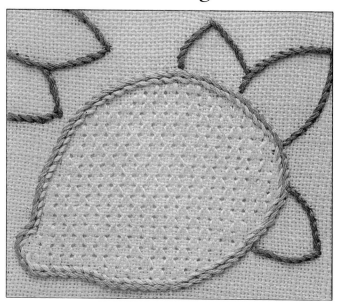

Materials Stranded cotton, coton à broder or linen thread for sharp pattern and outline.

Uses Bodice, motif and pocket detail for summer dress, corner motif for napkin set, trolley cover or buffet runner.

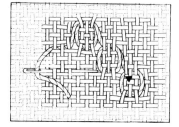

Begin at arrow and, working diagonally, encircle the groups of threads in threes to form one stitch before moving on to the next as shown. Turn work upside-down to work the next row, fitting the stitches closely into the spaces made by previous stitches.

Algerian eye stitch

Materials Mixed sewing threads, stranded silk, cotton, linen, or pearl thread for pretty posy pattern.

Uses Dress and jacket shoulder spray or négligé; corner motif for clutch bag, cushion set, trolley cloth or buffet runner.

Begin at arrow and work 8 straight stitches, each over 2 threads or any even number worked from the outer edge into the same central hole, as shown.

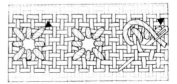

Three=sided stitch

Materials Stranded cotton, coton à broder or linen thread for clear stitch texture and graphic detail.

Uses "Home sweet home" picture, greetings or anniversary card or guest towel motif; "house" stitch sampler or cushion inset panel.

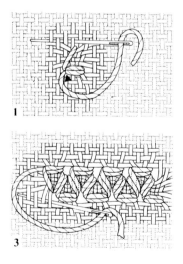

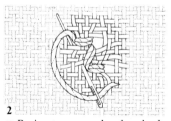

1 *Begin at arrow and make 2 back stitches to right over 4 threads. Bring needle out at starting point and make 2 more back stitches diagonally upwards to right over the same number of threads, bringing needle out 4 threads to left.*
2 *Work 2 back stitches. Then work 2 back stitches down to right.*
3 *Continue in this way, to end of row. Pull all stitches firmly.*

Four=sided stitch

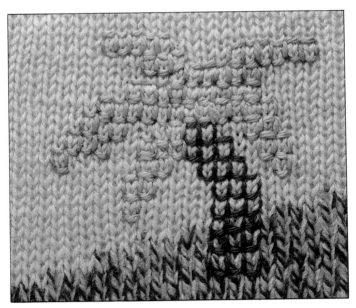

Materials Medium-weight stranded cotton, soft embroidery, lurex thread, tapestry or knitting yarn for stitch detail.

Uses Single motif for sweater, cardigan or pocket, scarf and hat or knitted cushion set.

1

2

3

1 *Insert needle 4 threads to left of arrow and bring out 4 threads below.*
2 *Insert needle at starting point, pass down and bring out 4 intersections to left.*
3 *Insert needle 4 threads up, pass down and bring out 4 intersections to right.*
4 *Repeat steps 1 to 3.*
5 *Work upwards into sides of previous row.*

4

5

Antique hem stitch

Materials Sewing threads, coton à broder or linen thread, to show off a simple hem.
Uses Table cloth and napkins, trolley cloth, buffet runner or window shade.

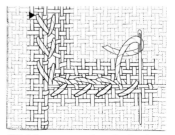

Withdraw 1 or 2 threads. Begin at arrow on wrong side of fabric. Pass needle to left under 3 vertical threads. Pull thread, insert needle into folded hem and bring out 2 threads down. Pull thread firmly ready for next stitch.

Trellis hem stitch

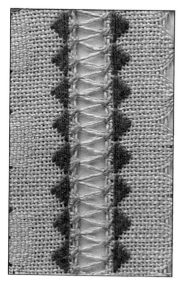

Materials Medium-weight stranded cotton, coton à broder or pearl thread for pretty open-stitched border.
Uses Kitchen or bathroom shade, pocket detail on linen skirt, tray or trolley cloth or table linen.

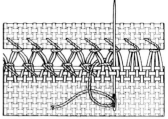

Withdraw several border threads. Hemstitch along top line in 4-thread clusters; the needle encircles 4 vertical threads before passing behind 2 threads of main fabric. Hemstitch along bottom line, starting with 2 threads, thus dividing upper clusters into pattern.

Knotted clusters

Withdraw required number of threads and hemstitch both sides of border. Draw every 3 clusters together with a knot by passing needle behind clusters and bringing it out through loop. Pull tight and repeat to end of border.

Materials Fine stranded silk or cotton, coton à broder, or sewing threads for a very lacy effect.
Uses Inset panel for nightdress or négligé, silk shirt, dress, pocket or cuff detail.

Single crossing clusters

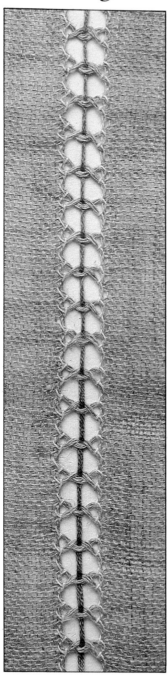

Materials Coton à broder, medium-stranded cotton, linen thread or withdrawn threads from ground fabric for a simple cluster pattern.

Uses Decorative hem for table linen or all-over repeat for cushion set or dress back panel.

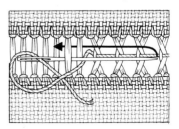

Withdraw required number of threads and hemstitch border with even clusters on both sides. Secure working thread centrally to fold line at right. Pass thread over 2 clusters and insert needle from left to right behind 2nd cluster, twist it back, inserting needle behind 1st cluster from right to left. Bring thread through, pulling firmly, ready to cross following 2 clusters.

Simple needleweaving

Materials Stranded cotton, coton à broder, pearl or linen thread for woven pattern effect.
Uses Lower single border for window shade, lampshade or buffet runner; all-over repeat for cushion (supported on a contrasting fabric).

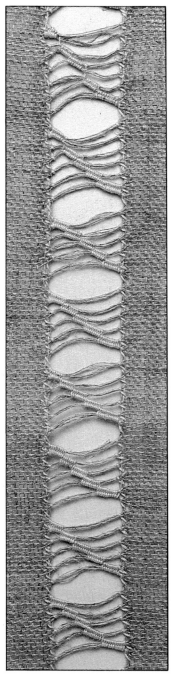

In needleweaving where the woven pattern completely covers the loose threads, hemstitching is not necessary. Withdraw required number of border threads. Begin at bottom right and work upwards weaving over and under pairs of 2 threads. At the top, pass the needle invisibly through the fabric to left ready to work the next column downwards, as in diagram.

For a more decorative finish, prepare border to required width, hemstitching both sides evenly in 3 thread clusters. The pattern consists of 5 evenly stepped blocks of stitches made diagonally across the loose threads. Begin at the top and following the above diagram, weave back and forth under and over 2 clusters for first block, and then pass needle under next cluster to left, ready to weave the next block. Work 5 blocks and finish off. Continue in this way to complete border pattern.

Patterned needleweaving

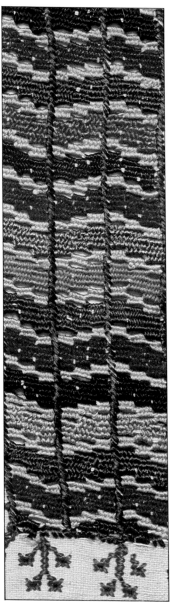

Materials Pearl thread, stranded cotton, coton à broder or linen thread for bright, woven effect; soft embroidery thread or knitting yarn for a chunky look.

Uses Dress inset panel, shoulder or pocket detail; peasant-style blouse yoke or sleeve detail.

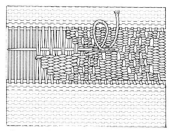

Prepare border to required width for woven pattern. Work the basic stitch as for simple needleweaving, closely interlocking each diagonal block of stitches worked in a variety of colors.

CUTWORK

This delicate and lacy form of embroidery consists of a combination of "cut away" areas and simple buttonhole stitching. Successful cutwork depends on a well-planned design: having all major points attached to avoid free-hanging sections when the background area is cut away. Delicately shaped flowers and leaves, linked with tiny stitched bars, contrast with scallop and leafy-shaped edges and eyelet patterns.

Buttonhole edge

Materials Coton à broder, sewing threads, or stranded cotton for pretty shaping.

Uses Light summer dress neck edging, sleeve or skirt hem motif; border for light-weight bed jacket, petticoat or pajama top.

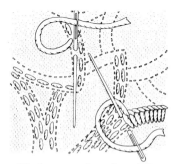

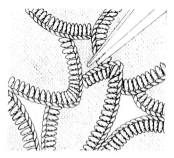

1 *Work 2 rows of running stitch between the double lines of the design. Cover with buttonhole stitch, keeping looped edge to inside.*

2 *When complete, work from wrong side and cut away background fabric as near to buttonhole edging as possible.*

Buttonhole bars

Materials Very fine stranded cotton, or sewing threads for delicate pattern linking.
Uses Corner motif for table napkin, trolley cloth or pajama sachet; back central point of deep collar, pocket or cuffs.

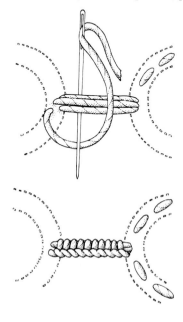

Work running stitch around the motif until a single bar is reached. Take the thread 3 times back and forth over the space and secure with a small stitch. Buttonhole stitch over the loose threads without picking up ground fabric, and then continue to work running stitch around the motif until the next bar is reached.

Scallop edge

Materials Pearl, stranded cotton, coton à broder or linen thread for firm, clear shaping.
Uses Edge feature on linen coat, pocket or sleeve; window shade or bedroom curtain ties.

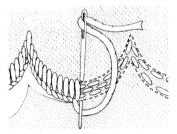

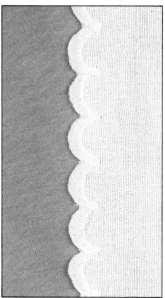

Mark pattern onto fabric, stitch outline and then work 2 rows of running stitch between the double lines. Buttonhole stitch closely over outlines, shaping stitches to fit scallop. Finally, cut away outer fabric close to stitch.

Oval edge

Materials Fine stranded cotton, silk or sewing threads for decorative points.
Uses Nightdress hem or silky pajama edging; lower edge of lampshade, window blind or buffet runner.

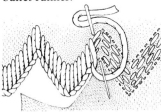

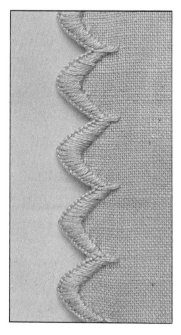

Mark pattern onto fabric, stitch outline and work 2 or 3 rows of running stitch between lines. Work buttonhole stitch closely around edge and cut outer fabric away.

Shamrock edge

Materials Pearl, coton à broder, stranded silk or cotton thread for deep, leafy edging.

Uses Circular tablecloth, oval tray cloth or trolley cover edging; corner motif for collar or lower edge of négligé.

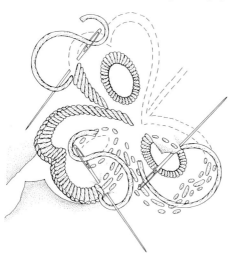

Mark pattern onto fabric. Stitch outline and work rows of running stitch between. Work buttonhole stitch around edge, completing each shamrock before working eyelets. Cut away outer fabric and eyelet centers.

Oval eyelets

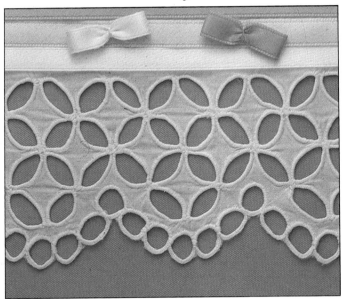

Materials Fine sewing thread, silk or stranded cotton for sharp, detailed effect.

Uses Négligé pocket trim, nightdress neck edge, baby's crib flounce or curtain ties for girl's room.

1 Mark pattern onto fabric and work running stitches around outlines. Snip center of eyelets and turn fabric back.
2 Overcast around each eyelet, making longer stitches at each end. Cut away fabric from inside eyelet, working from back.

Buttonholed eyelets

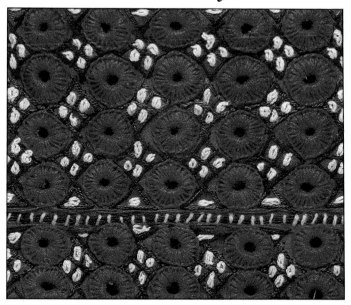

Materials Pearl, coton à broder, stranded cotton, lurex or linen thread for a colorful effect.

Uses Floor-cushion inset panel or bolster border; all-over repeat for shoulder bag, cushion set, or vest.

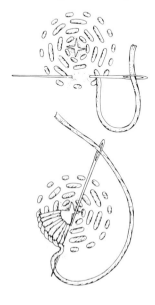

Mark position of eyelets onto fabric. Work running stitch around outer edge of each circle. Snip center, turn fabric to back and work close buttonhole stitch around edge. Keep looped edge of stitch to outer edge of eyelet and pull each stitch firmly.
Further embroidery stitches may be added between eyelets.

BEAD & SEQUIN

Sewn into your clothes – leather or knitted garments, fashion accessories or items for your home – a simple spray of beads or sequins can add just the right amount of color or dazzle. The stitch techniques for doing this are easy and quick to work, especially in a frame (see p.9), and include many fascinating effects, from beads on denim, bugles on bouclé, to silver kid with pearl sequins, zigzags of matt sequins with russia braid to bright shiny shisha glass.

Couching beads

Materials Small, regular-sized beads in a variety of colors and silk or linen thread (waxed) for a Sioux pattern.
Uses Border repeat for belt, blouson yoke or jeans pocket; denim bag or espadrille motif.

Bring needle out and thread on required number of beads. Slide 1st bead into position and with a separate needle and thread encircle thread to be couched close to the bead. Slide 2nd bead up to first and stitch as before. Continue in this way until all beads have been couched into position.

Stitching beads

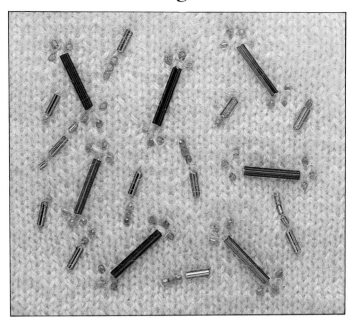

Materials Small, even-shaped glass beads and long bugle beads in mixed colors, with matching silk thread for random sparkle.
Uses Dress or sweater shoulder motif, cardigan front and pocket, glove or knee-sock detail.

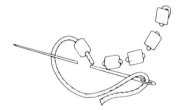

Bring needle out and thread bead onto it. Insert needle back through the same hole, make a stitch slightly longer than the bead, and pull through with thread below needle. Alternatively, make a stitch the length of the bead so that the next bead will touch the previous one.

Beads and sequins

Materials Mixed colored sequins, small beads and matching sewing threads for added dazzle.
Uses Shirt or blouson motif, cushion inset panel, or border repeat for bedspread and matching pillows.

Bring the needle out through the eye of the sequin and thread on a small bead, then insert the needle back through the eye of the sequin and pull tight so that the bead rests firmly over the eye, securing the sequin.

Invisible sequin stitch

Materials Sequins in two colors, metallic kid oddments and matching sewing threads for a classic look.

Uses Evening dress shoulder spray, clutch bag or belt motif; shawl corner or border repeat.

Bring needle through and thread on 1st sequin. Insert needle to left, close to edge of sequin, and bring out the same distance to left. Thread on 2nd sequin and work a back stitch into the left side of the 1st sequin to emerge as shown in diagram. Place sequin so that the right edge covers the eye of the previous one. Continue to work in this way.

Single back stitch

Materials Mixed colored sequins, beads and matching sewing threads for a pretty border.
Uses Border repeat for cardigan front, and pocket, evening shawl or cape; dress yoke, sleeve detail or cushion trim.

Bring needle through and thread sequin onto it. Work a back stitch over right side of sequin and bring needle out to left, ready to thread on next sequin which is placed edge to edge with the previous one.

Back stitch

Materials Sequins in three colors and matching sewing threads for a very smart finish.
Uses Dress hem or bodice trim, belt or pocket detail; diagonal border for envelope purse flap or evening wrap.

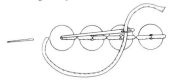

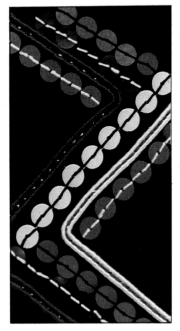

Work back stitch over right side of sequin. Bring needle out close to left edge of sequin and work a 2nd back stitch through the eye of the sequin. Bring needle out to far left, as shown in diagram, ready to stitch next sequin, which is placed edge to edge with the previous one. Continue in this way.

Shisha stitch

Materials Shisha glass or large sequins, coton à broder, pearl or linen thread for an Indian mirrored effect.

Uses Peasant-style dress inset panel; all-over repeat for waistcoat front, belt, bag or stitch sampler for patchwork quilt.

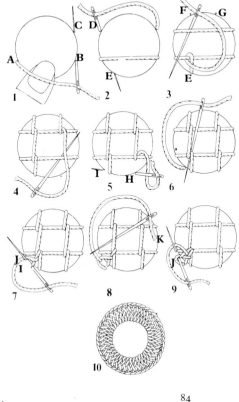

1 *Hold disc on surface of fabric with left thumb. Bring needle out at A. Carry thread to right over disc, make stitch BC.*

2 *Carry thread across disc, insert needle at D, and bring out at E.*

3 *Pass needle under 1st thread. Draw through, pass under 2nd thread; make stitch FG.*

4 *Pass needle under threads, as before.*

5 *Make stitch HI.*

6 *Pass needle under 1st intersection and bring out to right of working thread.*

7 *Make stitch IJ.*

8 *Pass needle under vertical thread and bring over working thread.*

9 *Make stitch JK.*

10 *Repeat steps 8 and 9 until disc is covered.*

COUCHING

Couching stitches, worked with a continuous thread, are best used for filling large motifs and backgrounds, whereas the best technique for working a bold unbroken line is where the main thread lies on the surface of the fabric and is held in place with a finer thread. Worked in a frame (see p.9), the line may be a single thread of silk or heavy metallic cord couched in a regular pattern with a matching or contrasting colored thread. Couched effects include broad and circular infilling, outlining and criss-crossed trellising.

Romanian couching

Materials Medium- to heavy-weight pearl thread, stranded cotton or mixed sewing thread for smooth-textured infilling.
Uses Kaftan or dressing gown inset panel, cushion set or bolster border, bag, belt or suspenders.

Bring needle through at left. Carry thread across area to be filled and secure with a single stitch at right, with thread above needle. On return journey, work fairly loose sloping stitches to end, bringing needle out ready to make next stitch.

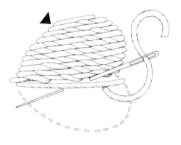

Bokhara couching

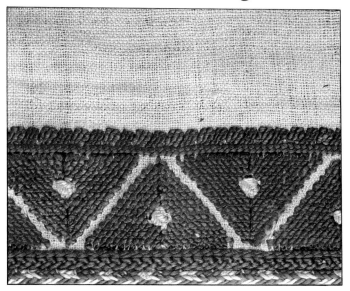

Materials Medium-weight pearl, silk or stranded cotton for fast, rib-textured infilling.

Uses Floor-cushion inset panel, curtain border or all-over repeat for waistcoat or shoulder bag.

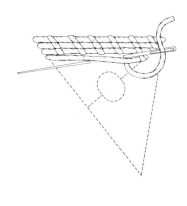

Bring needle out to left, carry thread to right and secure with a small stitch at right. Work as for Romanian stitch but make shorter tying stitches, which should be worked in a regular pattern.

Single line couching

Materials Fine silk, cotton, pearl or metallic thread for light out-lining; soft embroidery, pearl, lurex or cord threads for heavy fabrics.
Uses Padded jewel-box, greetings card or keepsake picture motif; padded workbox lid, wall panel or jeans jacket.

Bring out thread to be couched and hold along stitch line. Then, with a 2nd needle and thread, tie down the laid thread at regular intervals with small couching stitches. The tying stitch may be of a contrasting color.

Open filling

Materials Stranded silk or cotton, coton à broder or sewing thread for fun flowers; soft embroidery, crewel wool, knitting yarn or lurex for heavy duty.

Uses Motif for dress yoke and pocket, baby's carriage or crib cover; sweater, T-shirt, cardigan front and pocket or espadrille detail.

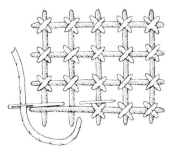

Make long evenly spaced stitches in both directions across the fabric. Then, with the same or contrasting color, tie down the laid threads with cross stitches worked over each intersection.

Couching with fly stitch

Materials Stranded silk or cotton, sewing thread, coton à broder or lurex for decorative couching.

Uses Wedding anniversary or birthday card motif, picture panel or blazer pocket "badge".

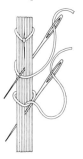

Bring out several threads placed evenly side by side (not through the same hole). Lay them along stitch line, and, with a 2nd needle, bring out a finer thread to top left. Work fly stitch over all threads in a regular pattern, as shown.

89

Circular filling

Materials Round gold thread (or any metallic imitation), matching sewing threads with colored silk or cotton embroidery thread for a very special look.

Uses Dress bodice inset panel or vest front; all-over repeat for evening bag or book cover.

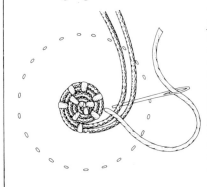

Working from the front of the fabric, insert ends of 2 metal cords into fabric at center of circle and secure at back with cotton thread. Bring out couching thread, encircle the cords with a small stitch close to the end and take needle to back, pulling firmly. Begin to coil the cords into a circle, keeping them flat and close together. Make regular tying stitches and continue in this way to complete circle. Cut ends of cord, take through to back and secure as before.

BRAID & RIBBON WORK

*Braid and ribbon work is a very simple and effective
form of decoration. The contrasting textures of velvet,
silk and satin ribbons, bindings and lace combine well with
plaited braids, cords and embroidery threads. You might
be inspired to work your own ideas based on the simple
techniques shown here. You will see how very easy it is to
apply an interlaced knot or monogram, or to build up a
pretty picture, a posy of roses or a fine lacy trim.*

Celtic knot

Materials Russia braid and matching sewing threads for a simple
interlacing effect.

Uses Motif for dressing gown or judo jacket; border repeat for satin
sheet and pillow cover or cushion set.

*Mark outline onto fabric and
starting in the center of knot, pin
and baste russia braid in place.
Begin with bottom right corner, as
shown, and when the knot is
complete, cut the braid and tuck
end under center crossing. With
matching sewing thread, use small
running stitches to stitch the knot
firmly in position. Remove basting
stitches.*

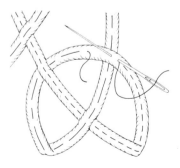

Window pane

Materials Velvet ribbon, satin binding, russia braid and matching sewing threads for quick-to-work picture effect.

Uses House-shaped coffee-pot cosy, or work-bag with window pockets; keepsake picture or greetings card motif.

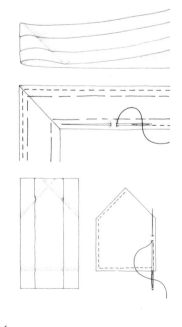

Mark guidelines for window frame onto background fabric. Baste russia braid in place and then floral bias binding, mitering corners, as shown in diagram. Apply outer velvet ribbon in the same way.

For window box, cut and fold satin binding to shape and baste in position. With matching thread, sew around all edges using small running stitches. Gather ribbon for pelmet and work flowers in mixed colors to complete window.

Rosy posy

Materials A variety of pink satin ribbons, green velvet ribbon and matching sewing threads for raised roses.

Uses Neckline posy for soft flowing dress, sash or shawl-corner detail; cushion inset panel.

Mark guidelines for posy onto fabric. For large roses, allow about 6in. × 1¼in. wide ribbon, and for small roses, 4in. × 1in. Join each piece into a circle and gather around bottom edge. Fold into a rose shape, and stitch to hold position. Make required number of roses and leaves. Cut and shape velvet ribbon for leaves, as for window box opposite. Gather center line for veins. Arrange posy and stitch firmly onto fabric.

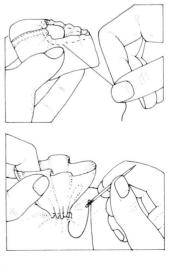

Lavender and lace

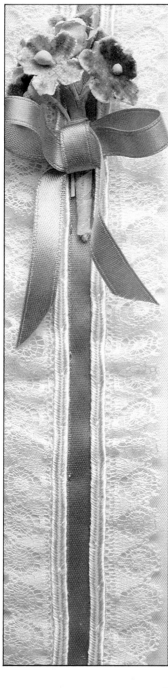

Materials Narrow ribbon, lace edging, russia braid, tiny artificial flowers and matching sewing threads for a soft, feminine look.
Uses Heart-shaped card or cushion trim; bedhead finish and matching pillow motif. (Remove flowers before hand-laundering.)

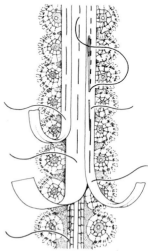

Cut required lengths of lace, russia braid and ribbon for depth of design. Cut additional ribbon for bows at top and bottom. Pin and baste onto the fabric the 2 outer pieces of lace, then the satin ribbon over central join, and 1 piece of russia braid to either side of it. Use matching thread and running stitches to sew in place, as shown. To finish, tie and stitch bows and arrange flowers, catching the stalks neatly under the bow.

Index

Acknowledgments

Contributors
Barbara Dawson
Soozi de Leon
Embroiderers' Guild
FRIDA Marketing Services
(London)
Sally Harding
Jane Iles
Jonathan Langley
Lis Mossery
Royal School
of Needlework (London)
Louise Stern
Janet Swift
Victoria and Albert Museum

Photographers
Ian O'Leary
Steve Oliver

Artist
John Hutchinson

Typesetting
Contact Graphics Ltd

Reproduction
F. E. Burman Ltd